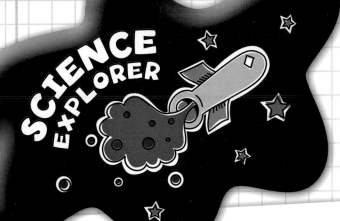

SCIENCE EXPLORER

SEEDS

SUPER COOL
SCIENCE
EXPERIMENTS:

by Susan H. Gray

CHERRY LAKE PUBLISHING • ANN ARBOR, MICHIGAN

CHERRY
LAKE
Publishing

A NOTE TO PARENTS AND TEACHERS: Please review the instructions for these experiments before your children do them. Be sure to help them with any experiments you do not think they can safely conduct on their own.

A NOTE TO KIDS: Be sure to ask an adult for help with these experiments when you need it. Always put your safety first!

Published in the United States of America by
Cherry Lake Publishing
Ann Arbor, Michigan
www.cherrylakepublishing.com

Content Editor: Robert Wolffe, EdD,
Professor of Teacher Education,
Bradley University, Peoria, Illinois

Book design and illustration: The Design Lab

Photo Credits: Cover and pages 1 and 7, ©Acik/Dreamstime.com;
page 5, ©iStockphoto.com/yucelyilmaz; page 8, ©iStockphoto.com/
skodonnell; page 12, ©Oliwkowygaj/Dreamstime.com; page 13,
©Artography/Dreamstime.com; page 18, ©iStockphoto.com/Scrambled;
page 20, ©iStockphoto.com/AVTG; page 24, ©Mikeexpert/Dreamstime.
com; page 27, ©Martin Shields/Alamy

Library of Congress Cataloging-in-Publication Data
Gray, Susan Heinrichs.
  Super cool science experiments : seeds / by Susan H. Gray.
    p. cm.—(Science explorer)
  Includes bibliographical references and index.
  ISBN-13: 978-1-60279-514-3   ISBN-10: 1-60279-514-2 (lib. bdg.)
  ISBN-13: 978-1-60279-593-8   ISBN-10: 1-60279-593-2 (pbk.)
  1. Seeds—Juvenile literature. 2. Seeds—Experiments—Juvenile
literature. I. Title. II. Series.
  QK661.G73 2009
  581.4'67—dc22   2008050538

Cherry Lake Publishing would like to acknowledge the work
of The Partnership for 21st Century Skills. Please visit
www.21stcenturyskills.org for more information.

SEEDS

TABLE OF CONTENTS

No Mad Scientists Here!

Super cool scientist

When you think of science, what comes to your mind? Do you think that experiments are difficult to do? Or that grown-up scientists are the only people who can do experiments?

Hopefully, you already know that science can be fun. You can do experiments with things you have at home. Anyone can think like a scientist. In this book, we'll learn how scientists think. We'll do that by experimenting with seeds. We don't need to be mad scientists to design our own experiments!

First Things First

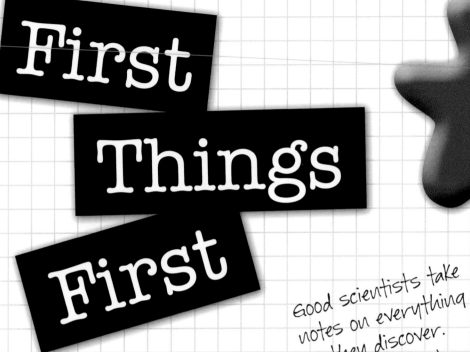

Scientists learn by studying things in nature very carefully. For example, scientists who study plants watch how they grow. They see which plants grow best in different areas. They notice which plants need a lot of water and which ones need only a little. They do experiments to see if seeds sprout best in warm weather or in cool weather. They try to figure out what kind of soil is best for each kind of plant.

Good scientists take notes on everything they discover. They write down their observations.

Sometimes those observations lead scientists to ask new questions. With new questions in mind, they design experiments to find the answers.

When scientists design experiments, they must think very clearly. The way they think about problems is often called the scientific method. What is the scientific method? It's a step-by-step way of finding answers to specific questions. The steps don't always follow the same pattern. Sometimes scientists change their minds. The process often works something like this:

Scientific method

- **Step One:** A scientist gathers all the facts and makes observations about one particular thing.
- **Step Two:** The scientist comes up with a question that is not answered by all the observations and facts.
- **Step Three:** The scientist creates a hypothesis. This is a statement of what the scientist thinks is probably the answer to the question.
- **Step Four:** The scientist tests the hypothesis. He or she designs an experiment to see whether the hypothesis is correct. The scientist does the experiment and writes down what happens.
- **Step Five:** The scientist draws a conclusion based on how the experiment turned out. The conclusion might be that the hypothesis is correct. Sometimes, though, the hypothesis is not correct. In that case, the scientist might develop a new hypothesis and another experiment.

In the following experiments, we'll see the scientific method in action. We'll gather some facts and observations about seeds. We'll develop a question and a hypothesis. Next, we'll come up with an experiment to see if our hypothesis is correct. We'll do the experiment. By the end of the experiment, we should know something new about seeds. Scientists, are you ready? Then let's get started!

Get your notebook ready and let's learn about seeds!

Experiment #1

Seeds' Needs

← What do you think the seeds in this field needed to grow?

First, let's gather some observations. What do you already know about seeds? You probably know that farmers keep an eye on the weather. They plant seeds when the temperature is right for the kind of plant they want to grow. Many seeds need warm temperatures to grow. Some grow best in cool weather. You may also know that seeds need water to germinate, or sprout.

These observations lead us to a question. **Do seeds need anything other than the correct temperature and enough water to germinate?** What do you think?

Maybe you are thinking that seeds might also need air to germinate. You decide that this is what you want to find out. So your hypothesis for the first experiment is this: **Seeds also need air to germinate.**

Now you can set up an experiment to test the hypothesis.

Here's what you'll need:
- 2 identical glass jars, labeled Jar #1 and Jar #2
- Water
- Paper towels
- Several kinds of dried beans from the grocery store. You can use pinto beans, navy beans, great northern beans, lima beans, or red kidney beans.
- A warm spot such as a sunny windowsill or the top of a refrigerator toward the back
- 2 identical boxes big enough to cover the jars

Make sure your jars are clean and clearly labeled.

Instructions:

1. Drop 10 assorted beans into Jar #1. Fill the jar to the top with water. Place that jar in a warm spot, and cover it with a box.

2. Next, moisten several paper towels (very damp, but not dripping). Wad them up, and place them loosely in Jar #2. Put 10 assorted beans in that jar. Place them between the glass and the wet paper towels so you can easily see them. Put this jar near Jar #1, and cover it with the other box.

3. Look at the beans the next day. If the water level is lower in the first jar, add more water. If the paper towels are getting dry, sprinkle some water on them. Have the beans changed at all? Look closely, and write down your observations.

Use damp paper towels in Jar #2.

4. Look at the beans the following day. Add water, if necessary, to the 2 jars. Have the beans changed since the day before? Are any of the beans sprouting? If so, which jar has the sprouting beans? Again, write down your observations. Observe the beans for 2 more days. Write down what you see.

Conclusion:

What can you conclude from this experiment? Did the underwater beans get any air? Did the beans need air to germinate? Was your hypothesis correct? Did the seeds also need sunlight to germinate? How do you know? Did they need soil to germinate? How do you know?

Crazy fact! →

Did you know that seeds have gone into outer space? That's right! Sometimes, astronauts take cases of seeds with them on the space shuttle. When they return to Earth, the seeds are sent to schools to be used in experiments. So far, millions of kids have done experiments on these space seeds. Can you think of some reasons why seeds would be sent into space?

Experiment #2

How Hot

Is Too Hot?

In Experiment #1, we learned that most seeds need warmth, water, and air to germinate. As a scientist, you might wonder just how much warmth is best. Maybe you are asking yourself this question: **If heat helps the seeds to germinate, will extreme heat help them germinate faster?**

So here's a new hypothesis: **Seeds that are boiled will germinate more quickly than seeds that are not boiled.** Time for another experiment.

You will need an adult to help you with part of this experiment.

Here's what you'll need:

- 2 identical glass jars, labeled 0 minutes and 10 minutes
- Paper towels
- Water
- A warm spot
- Saucepan
- Stove
- Clock or watch with a second hand
- Slotted spoon
- 20 dried lima beans

Instructions:

1. Put wet, loosely wadded paper towels in both jars. Place 10 dried beans in the "0 minutes" jar between the towels and the glass. Put this jar in a warm spot.

2. Have an adult help with the rest of this experiment. Put about 2 inches (5 centimeters) of water in the saucepan. Place the saucepan on the stove. Heat the water until it boils. Drop the 10 remaining beans into the boiling water.

Carefully drop the remaining 10 beans into the boiling water.

Look at the clock when the beans are added. After 10 minutes, turn off the heat. Use the slotted spoon to scoop out the beans from the pan. Let them cool off on a paper towel. Then place them between the wet paper towels and the glass in the "10 minutes" jar. Put the jar in a warm spot.

3. For the next few days, keep the paper towels damp and observe the beans. What do you see? Which beans germinated? Is that what you expected? Was your hypothesis correct? Why do you think this happened? How could you change this experiment to try to find out how much warmth is best for germination?

Don't let your feelings get in the way!

Sometimes, scientists let their feelings affect their thinking. They can't believe it when a hypothesis turns out wrong. They do their experiments over and over, hoping to get different results. When scientists let their feelings get in the way, they can't learn from their experiments. How about you? Were you disappointed when the hypothesis turned out to be wrong? Did you want to try the experiment again?

Experiment #3

Scarred for Life

← Place 10 assorted beans in a jar with a wet paper towel.

Before we do this experiment, let's look more closely at our seeds. Place 10 assorted beans in a jar with wet paper towels wadded up inside. Put the jar in a warm place. Observe the beans for the next 2 days. Remove them soon after they begin to germinate. Take a close look at them. What has happened to their hard outer covering? Are the seeds larger or smaller than they were before going into the jars? Why have they changed size?

The outer covering of the seed is called the seed coat. Pick the seed coat off one of the beans. Then run your thumbnail along the curved edge of the bean to split it in two. What do you find inside? When the bean germinates, does it send out a root or a stem?

You probably noticed that the seed coat was easy to pull off. Water softened it up and caused it to wrinkle and split. This allowed water to seep into the rest of the bean. As the bean soaked up water, it swelled and caused the seed coat to split even more. Could you speed up germination by damaging the seed coat to make it split more easily? That's a good question! It's time for another hypothesis and experiment. Here are some possible hypotheses. Read them, and pick the one you think is most likely to happen.

Hypothesis #1: Seeds with damaged outer coats will germinate more slowly than those with undamaged coats.

Hypothesis #2: Seeds with damaged outer coats will germinate faster than those with undamaged coats.

Hypothesis #3: The condition of the seed coat won't make any difference in how quickly the seed sprouts.

You will need one piece of fine sandpaper.

Clearly label two clean jars as "Sanded" and "Not Sanded."

Here's what you'll need:

- 2 identical glass jars, labeled "Sanded" and "Not Sanded"
- Water
- Paper towels
- 20 dried beans, all of the same kind
- A warm spot
- Fine sandpaper

Lightly sand 10 beans on both sides and put them in the "Sanded" jar.

Instructions:

1. Prepare the two glass jars as before, with damp paper towels. Place 10 beans in the "Not Sanded" jar and put it in the warm spot. Lightly sand the remaining 10 beans on both sides. Put them in the "Sanded" jar, and place that jar in the warm spot.

2. Keep the paper towels damp, and observe the beans several times a day during the next 3 days. Which beans germinated more quickly? Was your hypothesis correct?

Gardeners often use this trick to speed up germination. Some flower seeds have very hard outer coats. Smart gardeners will scrape away part of the coat. Then they keep the seeds in a damp container for a day before planting.

Experiment #4
Roots Know What They're Doing

In what direction do you think the roots to this tree are growing? —→

Look outside at the grass, bushes, and trees. How many do you see with their roots growing up toward the sun? Have you ever seen any growing plant with all of its roots reaching upward? No? Then your observations tell you that roots grow down into the ground.

Now think back to what you've already seen in your experiments. The seeds in the jars sprouted roots in all directions. At first, some roots pointed upward, some downward, and some to the left and right. As a scientist, you might ask, "Do roots eventually grow downward no matter which direction the seeds point?"

If your answer to this question was yes, your hypothesis would be: **It doesn't matter in which direction you aim the seeds. Roots will grow downward.** Time to experiment!

Here's what you'll need:
- A 2-liter clear plastic soda bottle, with the narrowed top cut off
- A cup of marbles or small gravel
- A square of nylon net or cheesecloth, measuring about 18 inches (46 cm) on each side
- Potting soil
- Marking pen
- 12 dried beans of one kind
- A warm spot

Ask an adult to help cut off the top of the plastic soda bottle.

Instructions:

1. Place the marbles or gravel in the bottom of the plastic bottle. Fold the nylon net or cheesecloth several times and place it on top of the gravel. This will let excess water drain to the bottom of the bottle. Fill the bottle almost to the top with potting soil. Mark an arrow that points down on one side of the bottle. Turn the bottle a quarter turn, and mark a left-pointing arrow. Turn it another quarter turn, and mark an arrow that points up. Turn it one more quarter turn, and mark a right-pointing arrow. You should now have four different arrows on four sides of the bottle.

Each side of your plastic bottle should be clearly marked with an arrow.

A seed's hilum
is like your
belly button.

2. Find the hilum on each
   bean. This is the scar where
   the bean was once attached
   to the bean pod. On the side
   with the up arrow, plant
   three beans with the hilum
   pointing up. Plant them about
   1 inch (2.5 cm) deep. Place them right against
   the plastic so you can see them. Plant three more
   beans with the hilum pointing left on the side
   with the left arrow. On the side with the down
   arrow, plant three beans with the hilum pointing
   down. On the side with the right arrow, plant the
   last three beans with the hilum pointing to the
   right. Place the bottle in a warm spot. Keep the
   soil moist but not soaking wet.
3. Observe the beans for the next week. When they
   begin to germinate, in what direction do the roots
   point? At the end of the week, which way do they
   point? What does this tell you about roots?

Don't throw out the bottle and seeds yet. You'll need
them for the next experiment.

Experiment #5
Can Roots
Be Fooled?

↶These grass roots
have all grown downward.

In Experiment #4, you observed that roots will grow
downward. It does not matter how the seeds are
planted. Perhaps there is something in the roots
that makes them grow downward. If that is true,
then roots should grow downward, no matter what.

Hypothesis: Even if you turn the germinating plants in another direction, the roots will continue to grow downward.

Let's test the hypothesis.

Here's what you'll need:
- The soda bottle containing the 12 young plants from the last experiment
- A warm spot
- A thick book, a block of wood, or a brick to lean the bottle against
- Tape

Besides the items here, you will need your notebook so you can record what happens each day. →

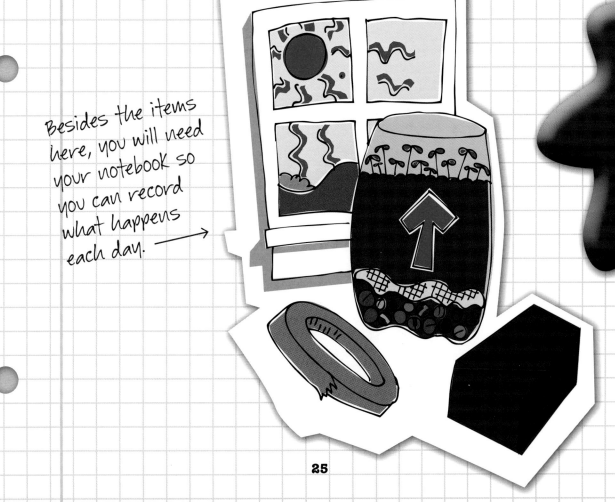

Instructions:

1. Keep the soda bottle in the warm spot. Lean it over so the upper edge rests on the book or block. Rotate the bottle so that one set of seeds is showing on the upper surface of the bottle, one set on the lower surface, and one set on each side. You may have to tape the bottle in place to keep it from rolling.

2. Keep the soil damp, and continue to observe the roots for another week. If you stand the bottle up to add water, be sure to return it to the exact same position. What happens to the roots during the week? Is your hypothesis correct?

As you observe throughout the week, take careful notes.

Other scientists have noticed this same thing in plants. They have investigated the substances inside roots. They have found chemicals that affect how fast plant cells grow. These chemicals are called auxins.

Auxins cause root cells to grow more slowly. Gravity causes the auxins to trickle down to the cells on the lower side of the roots. There they slow the cells' growth. The cells on the upper side of the root contain less auxin. So they grow more quickly. When the upper side of a root grows quickly and the lower side grows slowly, the root grows to bend downward.

Auxins, which ——→ cause the roots of a plant to grow down, also cause a plant to grow upward.

Experiment #6

Do It Yourself!

Some gardeners talk to their plants and encourage them to grow. They tell the seeds how great they look. They compliment the plants on how well they're doing. They say that seeds germinate better when they are treated with kindness.

Tell one of your plants how well it is growing and how beautiful it is.

Talk to Me!

Do you think these people are correct? To find out, set up an experiment. What is your hypothesis? What materials would you need to run the experiment? Write out the instructions for your experiment. Should you have 2 sets of seeds—one treated kindly and one not? Tell how you would show kindness to your plants. Decide how to judge whether your plants are responding. Do the experiment and write down what you find out.

Give the other plant the same amount of water and sunlight, but don't say anything to it.

No Talking

Okay, scientists! Now you know many new things about seeds. You learned through your observations and experiments. And in that last experiment, you probably felt a little goofy being kind to plants. Maybe scientists are just a little mad after all!

auxins (AWK-sinz) substances inside plants that affect cell growth

cells (SEHLZ) the smallest living units that make up plants and animals

conclusion (kuhn-KLOO-zhuhn) a final decision, thought, or opinion

germinate (JUR-muh-nayt) to sprout or begin to grow

hilum (HY-luhm) the scar on a seed showing where it attached to the parent plant

hypothesis (hy-POTH-uh-sihss) a logical guess about what will happen in an experiment

method (METH-uhd) a way of doing something

observations (ob-zur-VAY-shuhnz) things that are seen or noticed with other senses

BOOKS

Ardley, Neil. *101 Great Science Experiments.* New York: DK Publishing, 2006.

Benbow, Ann, and Colin Mably. *Lively Plant Science Projects.* Berkeley Heights, NJ: Enslow Elementary, 2009.

Benbow, Ann, and Colin Mably. *Sprouting Seed Science Projects.* Berkeley Heights, NJ: Enslow Elementary, 2009.

WEB SITES

Nutrition in the Garden: Gardening Ideas

aggie-horticulture.tamu.edu/nutrition/ideas/actnig.html

A few activities that show different features of seeds

Park Seed Memories—Rhode Island Kids Experiment with Seeds in Space

www.parkseedmemories.com/2008/05/rhode-island-ki.html

A story about a school in Rhode Island that experimented with seeds from a space shuttle

Zoom Activities—Sock Seeds

pbskids.org/zoom/activities/sci/sockseeds.html

A fun demonstration showing the different plants that exist in different environments

INDEX

About the →
Author

Susan H. Gray has a master's
degree in zoology. She has
written more than 100 science
and reference books for children,
and especially loves writing
about biology. Susan also likes to
garden and play the piano. She
lives in Cabot, Arkansas, with her
husband, Michael, and many pets.

No
Talking